AFFIRMING CATHOLICISM

———

Jeffrey John

'PERMANENT, FAITHFUL, STABLE'

Christian Same-sex Partnerships

———

Series Editor: Mark Oakley

DARTON·LONGMAN+TODD

First published in 1993 by
Darton, Longman and Todd Ltd
1 Spencer Court
140–2 Wandsworth High Street
London SW18 4JJ

in association with

Affirming Catholicism
St Matthew's House
20 Great Peter St
London SW1P 2BU

This edition published in 2000

Reprinted 2003 and 2004

© 1993 and 2000 Jeffrey John

ISBN 0–232–52364–9

Phototypeset by Intype London Ltd
Printed and bound in Great Britain by
Page Bros, Norwich

Affirming Catholicism

Affirming Catholicism is a movement (not an ecclesiastical party) which exists to do two things. We affirm our confidence in our Anglican heritage; and we seek to renew and promote the Catholic tradition within it. Our aim is to explore, explain and share with others both inside and outside the Church a lively, intelligent and inclusive Catholic faith. In the words of our Trust Deed:

> It is the conviction of many that a respect for scholarship and free enquiry has been characteristic of the Church of England and of the Churches of the wider Anglican Communion from earliest times, and is fully consistent with the status of those Churches as part of the Holy Catholic Church. It is desired to establish a charitable educational foundation which will be true both to those characteristics and to the Catholic tradition within Anglicanism ... The object of the foundation shall be the advancement of education in the doctrines and the historical development of the Church of England and the Churches of the wider Anglican Communion, as held by those standing within the Catholic tradition.

Our Publications

These are offered as one means of presenting Anglican Catholic teaching and practice in as clear and accessible a form as possible. Some cover traditional doctrinal and liturgical themes; others attempt to present a well-argued Catholic viewpoint on issues of debate currently facing the Church.

The present series of books is provided, where appro-priate, with summaries to sections, and suggested questions which we hope will facilitate personal study or discussion in groups. A list of publications available is given on page v. To order these publications individually or on subscription, or for further information about the aims and activities of Affirming Catholicism, write to:

> The Secretary
> Affirming Catholicism
> St Matthew's House
> 20 Great Peter St
> London SW1P 2BU
>
> Tel 020 7222 5166

Books in the Affirming Catholicism series

Affirming Confession John Davies
Anglican Orders and the Priesting of Women Paul Avis
By What Authority? Mark D Chapman
Catholic Evangelism Stephen Cottrell
Catholicism and Folk Religion Jeremy Morris
Christian Feminism Helen Stanton
Christ in Ten Thousand Places Michael Ipgrave
History, Tradition and Change Peter Hinchliff
Humanity and Healing Martin Dudley
Imagining Jesus Lewis Ayres
Introducing Richard Hooker Martyn Percy
Is the Anglican Church Catholic? Vincent Strudwick
Is There an Anglican Way? Ross Thompson
Lay Presidency at the Eucharist Benedict Green
Making a Rule of Life John Gaskell
Making Present Christopher Irvine
Marriage, Divorce and the Church Anthony Harvey
The Ministry of Deliverance Dominic Walker
Politics and the Faith Today Kenneth Leech
The Practice of Abortion Michael Banner
Trinity and Unity Jane Williams
What is Affirming Catholicism? Jeffrey John
Why Women Priests? Jonathan Sedgewick

About the Author

Jeffrey John is Canon Chancellor and Theologian of Southwark Cathedral, and a member of the executive committee of Affirming Catholicism.

He is the editor of *Living Tradition: Affirming Catholicism and the Anglican Church*, *Living Evangelism: Affirming Catholicism and Sharing the Faith*, *Living the Mystery: Affirming Catholicism and the Future of Anglicanism*, and *This Is Our Faith: Anglican Church Teaching for Adults*.

CONTENTS

Introduction

This booklet has a straightforward aim. It argues that homosexual relationships should be accepted and blessed by the Church, provided that the quality and commitment of the relationship are the same as those expected of a Christian marriage. It argues that the theological, ethical and sacramental status of such a partnership between two men or two women is comparable to that of a marriage, whether or not the word marriage is used to describe it. It also argues that the self-discipline and self-sacrifice which are required to make Christian marriage a way of holiness are equally required of a homosexual partnership which deserves the name Christian.

The title of this booklet 'Permanent, Faithful, Stable' is taken from the description of such a relationship in the Gloucester Report of 1979. This was the first Church of England report – though it was never officially ratified – to urge recognition of gay relationships by the Church. The phrase has become something of a cliché, but it says what needs to be said about the kind of relationship I want to defend.

The view which is put forward in this booklet tends to draw fire from both sides of the argument.

On the one hand, many Christians, perhaps still the majority, hold on the grounds of Scripture and tradition that no kind of homosexual practice is compatible with Christian discipleship. This is the official view of the Roman Catholic Church, the Orthodox

Churches and most of the Protestant Churches (though it is important to distinguish the official view from the private views of the leadership of these Churches, especially in the West). The Lambeth Conference of the Bishops of the Anglican Communion in 1998 also confirmed the traditionally negative stance, and declared that all homosexual practice is 'incompatible with scripture'. Lambeth Conference resolutions, however, are not binding on member churches. The official position of the Church of England is expressed in the Statement *Issues in Human Sexuality*, published by the English bishops in 1991 and belatedly endorsed by General Synod in 1997. The Statement is a more nuanced document, which at certain points hovers on the edge of acceptance, urging congregations to accept and support Christians who conscientiously believe themselves to be called to live in faithful partnership. However, the overall tone remains hesitant and grudging, insisting that a gay relationship 'falls short' of the ideal of Christian marriage; and for this reason the Statement forbids such a relationship to clergy, because of their 'exemplary' role. Since *Issues in Human Sexuality* remains the most authoritative pronouncement to date in the Church of England on the subject of homosexuality, it will be referred to fairly frequently in what follows.

On the other hand, the view put forward in this booklet is opposed by some gay people, including some of the most active and vocal, who think that for homosexuals to adopt a monogamous model of relationship (sometimes dismissed as 'coupledom') is an inappropriate aping of heterosexual marriage. In recent years, partly because of the threat of AIDS, the idea and practice of exclusive partnership and sexual fidelity have gained more currency in gay circles. Long-term same-sex partnerships are much more visible in the media, and a number of countries have accorded them civil and legal recognition. It is questionable, however, to what extent this trend has any moral or ideological basis. Andrew Sullivan, one of the most intellectually substantial of contemporary gay writers, argues powerfully for gay – and straight – monogamy on psychological, social and political grounds, but his views are hotly contested in gay circles. In the past even gay Christian organizations have been unwilling to formulate a monogamous ethic. Much has been said and written about the need to find a theological model for gay relationships, but in some quarters there has been a marked reluctance to apply the obvious one. This reluctance is certainly due in part to the negative image of marriage for some gay people, perhaps especially among lesbians, for whom the concept of monogamy often seems to carry an inseparable connotation of male dominance. Perhaps another reason is an instinctive fear of seeming to apply 'rules', when the Church's and society's rules are perceived as so unjust and repressive.

So I have to argue on two fronts.

First, I want to help convince the mainstream Church that a faithful homosexual relationship is not 'incompatible with scripture' (certainly no more so than the remarriage of the divorced, or the leadership of women, which are far more 'incompatible' with the Bible's plainest meaning). I want to make it clear that

accepting such a relationship does not mean jettisoning the traditional, biblical theology of sex and
marriage, but rather extending it to include gay people
– just as the sacrament of holy order has been
extended in the Anglican Church to include women,
without at all changing our underlying theology of
ministry. What makes a marriage sacramental is its
nature as a faithful covenant, which expresses God's
likeness in us and reflects the love between Christ
and his Church. I want to persuade all Christians that
a same-sex partnership based on the same commitment is no less sacramental, no less a way of holiness,
and no less worthy of the Church's blessing.

At the same time I want to persuade gay people
that contrary to the usual assumptions, the gospel has
something positive to say about gay relationships, and
that those who live in them belong in the Church as
much as anyone else. I want to point out that the
sacramental theology which underlies the Church's
teaching about sex and marriage applies to all human
beings made in God's image, not just to heterosexuals.
This theology says that human sexuality is not exclusively or necessarily intended for procreation; it is also
intended to express a covenant commitment between
two people which is holy because it reflects God's
covenanted love for us, and gives us a framework for
learning to love in his image. It means that for two
people, whether of the same or different sexes, to live
in such a faithful covenant with each other is a way
to greater freedom and growth, not a death-dealing
rule. I want to hold out the hope, inspiration and
moral challenge that such an understanding implies. I
also want to strengthen Christian gay couples who

already understand this, and know that their relationship is God's gift and vocation for them, but who have to struggle to stay in a Church which repeatedly insults and rejects them.

I would not dare to write about the theology of Christian gay relationships if I did not know that it works. What I am writing derives as much from personal and pastoral experience as from theological reflection. Knowledge of many relationships based on this kind of Christian understanding and commitment has proved to me that it is not naive or impracticable. Of course there is no such thing as the perfect Christian gay relationship, any more than one can point to the perfect Christian marriage. One of the wiser things Archbishop Runcie said in the infamous General Synod debate of 1987 was that 'in this earthly tabernacle of Christ's kingdom there are many mansions, and all of them are made of glass'. The truth is that in matters of sex and human relationship, heterosexual or homosexual, all of us 'fall short of the ideal'.

But that does not mean we should abandon the ideal, or pretend that it does not exist, or worse still, deny it to others. For most of my ministry I have worked with young adults in secular and theological colleges, and with young clergy. Many of them have been lesbian or gay, and many of them desperately struggling to reconcile their sexuality with membership of a hostile or uncomprehending Church. Almost all of them rejected promiscuity, and feared the futile prospect of a series of abortive relationships leading to a lonely old age. What they wanted was, precisely, the ideal: the hope, like their heterosexual friends, of finding someone to love and be wholly given to, someone to grow together with, someone who would still be there at the end of the day and at the end of their life. That is not a heterosexual hope or a homosexual hope; it is a fundamental human hope. To deny and subvert that hope is simply inhumane, and utterly un-Christian. I am writing this because I believe we have an absolute duty in the Church to offer homosexual couples a positive theological understanding of their relationship as well as practical acceptance and support, just as we offer both to heterosexual couples in marriage, to help them fulfil the same hope, the same ideal – of permanent, faithful, stable love.

Is It Scriptural?

'Incompatible with Scripture'?: Use and Abuse of the Bible

I have a vivid memory of spending an unhappy afternoon some years ago over a Bible trying to talk Simon out of attempting suicide again. Simon was a gay Evangelical student, totally convinced on the basis of Romans 1 that if he ever succumbed to his feelings he would be damned. He had consulted the vicar of his own church, who had promptly prayed for 'healing', and simultaneously ordered him to give up helping in the Sunday School, 'to protect the little boys'. Not surprisingly, Simon had come back to college and swallowed half a bottle of pills. It was particularly tragic for him, and still is for many gay Evangelicals, that so many would-be 'Bible Christians' seem to have made a hard line on this issue practically a test of faith. Fortunately, some Evangelicals are now protesting against this line, but a great deal of damage is still being done.

It is important to see how damaging it is to use the Bible to condemn homosexuals in this way. It is equally important to see how arbitrary and selective it is, and how false is the claim to genuine scriptural authority. In a notorious pronouncement, the Lambeth Conference of 1998 embraced exactly this kind of selective fundamentalism by declaring that all homosexual acts are 'incompatible with Scripture'. What can this phrase mean? As we shall see, Scripture's teaching on homosexuality is sparse and ambiguous, and it is highly questionable to what extent we can derive from it any application to the ethical issue of gay relationships as it faces us today. Yet this consideration did not prevent the bishops from issuing their blanket condemnation.

Contrast another ethical issue: that of divorce and remarriage. In four Gospel passages we are told that Jesus himself forbade the remarriage of the divorced as being equivalent to adultery. There is no doubt about the meaning of the words used, nor is there any indication that Jesus intended this teaching to be temporary or 'contextually interpreted'. On the contrary, it is a teaching he explicitly derives from God's plan in creation, and it is unambiguously expressed. Nothing of remotely equivalent weight and authority is stated in Scripture against homosexuality. How is it, then, that the Lambeth bishops can deny legitimacy, let alone blessing, to a faithful same-sex relationship on supposedly 'scriptural' grounds, yet, in the case of the great majority, are willing to bless remarried couples, and in some cases are divorced and remarried themselves? On what possible hermeneutical principle is 'incompatibility' discovered in the one case, yet not in the other? Let me emphasize that I do not use this example of remarriage in order to defend a literalist view on either issue. I use it because it demonstrates clearly that the bishops' declaration was based on prejudice, not on any consistent approach to biblical authority.

Similarly, why are so many Christians eager to take at face value what Paul says about homosexuals, but not what he says about women? Paul seems in three places (two only in passing) to condemn homosexual practice as sin. He has a great deal more to say about women. Consider his plain command that women must wear a head covering in church as a sign of their subordination; that women must be silent in the churches 'for they are not permitted to speak but must be silent as even the Law says'; that no woman may teach or hold authority over men, 'for Adam was formed first, then Eve; and Adam was not deceived, but the woman was deceived and became a transgressor. Yet woman will be saved through childbearing . . .'. In the social circumstances of today these passages, which are so plainly degrading to women, are highly embarrassing to 'Bible-based' churches. Paul himself lays far more stress on them than on his references to homosexuals. Yet in practice few even of the most so-called biblical churches now feel able to enforce the veiling of women or keep them silent.

If challenged on this, biblical conservatives will employ exactly the sort of arguments which on other matters, not least homosexuality, they condemn as 'getting round the plain meaning of Scripture' or 'capitulating to the spirit of the age'. In the case of Paul's teaching about women, they have to admit, when forced to the point, to making a distinction between temporary, 'culturally conditioned' teachings in certain passages, and wider biblical principles of justice and love with which those texts are now felt to conflict. Or else they will argue that Paul's teaching on women was conditioned by special circumstances in the churches he was writing to (though in fact more than once Paul says his teaching about women is binding on all the churches). The point to press home is that on such an issue even hard-line fundamentalists have been forced by outside moral pressure to recognize that certain biblical teachings must sometimes be weighed against other biblical principles and changed social conditions, and must sometimes be set aside. The sad truth is, the reason this has happened in the case of women and not in the case of homosexuals is that whereas prejudice against women is now much less tolerated in society at large, prejudice against homosexuals is still very much in force.

Sodom

Because so many Christians, even from Catholic and liberal traditions, still approach Scripture with essentially fundamentalist instincts, it is important to keep emphasizing that one cannot derive ethical instruction from the Bible texts without regard to their social and historical context and without weighing them against the thrust of Scripture as a whole. For example, even now one often hears the Sodom story (Genesis 19) brought into Christian arguments about homosexual practice. Yet, as has been shown many times, the story has no relevance whatsoever to the ethical issues surrounding homosexual relationships, and never did.

In the original story the 'sin of Sodom' for which God had already decided to destroy the city before the events at Lot's house is unspecified. The sin committed by all the men of Sodom at Lot's house was one of gang rape by a majority (presumably) of heterosexual men. The homosexual element in the act held no particular interest for the author (the violation of hospitality would have been counted a far worse category of crime). Indeed, for centuries afterwards the 'sin of Sodom' was perceived not as homosexuality but as the contravention of the rules of hospitality, as it was clearly understood by Jesus himself in Matthew 10:14–15.

The identification of the sin of Sodom with homosexuality was first made by Jewish commentators in the period between the Testaments, who had a special interest in condemning homosexuality as a typically Gentile vice. It was they who bequeathed to subsequent generations the quite false notion that God destroyed Sodom because of homosexuality, together with the offensive vocabulary of 'sodomy', 'sodomite' etc. One should also point out that it would be very strange for us to derive ethical guidance and moral insights from such a primitive story, a story in which it is assumed to be perfectly right for Lot to offer his two daughters to be raped by the crowd as substitutes for his male guests (Genesis 19:8). As the bishops' Statement notes, in such texts as this the situation is far too remote from our own in human terms for any ethical transfer to be made.

Leviticus

Something similar must be said about the prohibition of male homosexual behaviour in the Holiness Code of Leviticus, where it is punishable with death (18:22, 20:13). This is the earliest prohibition in Scripture, probably dating from the exile in Babylon, and it seems to have been conditioned by two main factors. First was the author's special concern to encourage childbirth in the situation of the exile and the forthcoming resettlement of Israel. (Probably the same author, known as the Priestly Writer, wrote the creation story in Genesis 1 with its command to 'go forth and multiply'.) Second was the need to counter syncretism by distinguishing sharply the ways of the Jews from those of the Gentiles. Babylonian society was apparently particularly tolerant of homosexual practice, and its worship may have involved homosexual activity. So by the ban on homosexuality the religious leaders of Israel sought to separate Jews from their Gentile captors – perhaps in more ways than one. It seems to have been this author who first labelled homosexuality as a particularly Gentile sin, and the abhorrence of it as a marker of Jewishness. Thereafter it becomes standard in Jewish literature to present homosexuality as characteristic of Israel's Gentile oppressors, and 'unknown in Israel'.

The Holiness Code is all about what sets Israel apart as holy to the Lord, but it is highly selective to single out homosexuality from the whole list of activities which it condemns as 'abominations' – a list which includes, for example, the trimming of one's beard, the consumption of shellfish and the weaving of two different kinds of yarn into the same garment. (The next time you see a clean-shaven fundamentalist wearing a poly-cotton shirt and eating a shrimp, remember to shout 'Abomination' and point this out!) Of themselves the Levitical rules are never regarded as having moral force for Christians, and Christians are not accustomed to look to them for guidance – except when seeking a text with which to beat homosexuals.

Paul

In the New Testament, the Gospels have nothing to
say about homosexuality. As far as we know, Jesus
never mentioned it. The only other relevant texts in
Scripture are in letters by Paul or attributed to him. In
1 Corinthians 6:9 and 1 Timothy 1:10 homosexuality
is mentioned in passing within conventional sin-lists,
probably taken over from Hellenistic Jewish sources.
(Both Hellenistic and Palestinian Judaism perpetu-
ated the Levitical attitude to homosexuality as a
Gentile vice associated with the worship of pagan
gods, and made extensive use of it as a piece of
religious and political propaganda.) There is some
reason to think that the words which we translate as
'homosexual' in these verses imply male prostitution,
but this cannot be pressed. What is far more important
is to remember that in the society in which Paul lived
prostitution and pederasty (in the sense of the Greek
practice of a temporary pupil-tutor relationship
between a teenager and an older man) were the standard forms of homosexual practice, and these are the
forms which were likely to be uppermost in Paul's
mind when he refers to homosexuals. One cannot
fairly make an ethical transfer from the assumptions
behind these verses to the kind of equal, adult
relationship which I am trying to defend in this
booklet. There is every reason to suppose that the
possibility of such a relationship never entered Paul's
thinking.

The most significant biblical text mentioning homosexuality is the one which drove Simon to despair:
Romans 1:18ff. This needs a little attention because
it is by far the most important text to be considered,

the only place where we have anything like a theological argument against homosexual practice.
However, the subject of homosexuality is not Paul's
real interest here. The epistle is addressed to a church
composed of both Jewish and Gentile converts. From
Romans 1:18 to the end of the chapter Paul is engaged
in an attack on Gentile idolatry. He argues that all
people could have deduced knowledge of God from
observing his creation, but they chose to reject that
knowledge and turned to idol worship (v. 23). Because
of this perverse rejection of him, therefore God abandoned them to their lusts and impurity (v. 24), to
dishonourable passions exemplified in the exchange
of heterosexual intercourse for homosexual (v. 25),
and to a base mind and improper conduct, exemplified
in a long list of sins deserving death which closes the
chapter (vv. 28–32). This completes the attack on
the Gentiles. The tables are then turned at the start
of chapter 2, where Paul rounds on the Jews in his
audience (who may well have been applauding smugly
up to this point) to condemn them equally for the
same sins, although they had even less excuse, having
the Law. The rhetorical pattern is carefully con-
structed, and reaches its climax in chapter 3 with the
fundamental proclamation that Paul wants to impress
on Gentiles and Jews alike: that all have sinned, none
is righteous, but all can be justified through the
atoning sacrifice of Jesus Christ.

The rhetorical force of the exercise lies in Paul's
quoting back at the Jews their own conventional
propaganda against the Gentiles. As we have seen,
both Palestinian and Hellenistic Judaism portrayed
homosexuality as an exclusively Gentile vice. In Hell-

enistic Judaism especially the homosexuality to which the Gentiles are supposed to incline is conventionally related to their idolatry, the moral 'exchange' of one sex for another being seen as the direct result of the religious 'exchange' of the true God for an idol. Paul repeats this standard argument; in fact several verses in the Book of Wisdom chapters 13 and 14 are sufficiently close to make borrowing a real possibility, and there are also parallels in Philo, Josephus and the Testament of the Twelve Patriarchs.

Of course the fact that Paul borrowed a piece of conventional anti-Gentile polemic need not undermine the authority of what he says, but there is another important point to be made about the presuppositions of his argument. When Paul argues that homosexuality is 'against nature' he does not only mean that it is against the order of nature itself, but also that it is against the person's *own* nature. Like all earlier and contemporary Jewish (though not all classical) writers on the subject, Paul does not recognize a separate category of homosexual people but only homosexual acts. He takes it for granted that homosexual behaviour is a free, perverse choice on the part of 'naturally' heterosexual men and women. This assumption is perfectly clear in his statements that homosexuals 'gave up' or 'exchanged' heterosexual relations in verses 26 and 27. It is also essential to his portrayal of homosexuality as an instance and reflection of idolatry. He must believe that homosexuals wilfully choose their unnatural aberration in the same way that he must believe that idolaters wilfully suppress the truth about God that must be known to them from observing creation (1:18–19).

Otherwise, as he says, God would not be just in his condemnation, and Paul could not say they are without excuse (1:20).

Yet we know now that this fundamental assumption on Paul's part is quite false. His belief that homosexual acts are committed by 'naturally' heterosexual people is untrue. There are quite clearly those whose exclusive or predominant inclination, whether for genetic reasons or reasons of upbringing, is unarguably and unchangeably towards their own sex. And as Paul himself admits, if men and women had no choice in the matter, God would hardly be just in condemning them. We may well agree with him, and observe that this false assumption on his part wholly undermines any blanket condemnation of homosexual practice on the basis of Romans 1.

It is, then, these two considerations: (1) that the object of Paul's condemnation was the model of homosexual practice in Hellenistic society, namely prostitution or pederasty, and (2) that neither Paul nor his Jewish antecedents considered the case of a homosexually orientated person, that make it thoroughly unjust to wield these texts against the kind of relationship I am seeking to defend.

Creation and Natural Law
Some will still argue that even a relationship of this quality must be condemned on the ground of Paul's so-called natural law objection that it is against the God-given pattern of creation. In an article defending this position one writer sums up such an argument with the comment that 'to accept homosexual acts by inverts would be to deny the doctrine of creation . . .

the whole biblical teaching on creation, sex, marriage, forgiveness and redemption will be fundamentally altered' (G. Wenham).

So let us consider the biblical argument from creation. What, scripturally speaking, is the purpose of sex? What was God's will in creating male and female? One might have assumed childbirth, but, surprisingly perhaps, in Genesis itself the primary reason that God created a companion for Adam is not said to be procreation, but because 'God said, "It is not good for man to be alone" ' (2:18). Complementarity and companionship are at least as much a part of God's plan in creation as childbirth. Indeed it is remarkable that in the Genesis account childbirth emerges only as an afterthought, and in the rather negative context of God's punishment of Eve (3:16). It is highly significant that Jesus and Paul, while both referring to the creation story, never once mention procreation or physical sexual difference in their teaching about marriage. On the contrary, their stress is entirely on the quality of the relationship, and in particular that it should be a covenant of total sexual fidelity and indissoluble union. Furthermore, the insistence on fidelity is never explained, as we might expect, with reference to practical reasons of child-bearing or domestic stability, but always with reference to the personal and spiritual implications of sexual union.

For Paul, sexual union *always* has spiritual consequences, whether for good or ill. Promiscuous sexual activity involves desecration of the body, which is a temple of the Spirit and itself a member of the Body of Christ (1 Corinthians 6:15–20). But where sexual union expresses mutual love and commitment, that relationship becomes a μυστήριον (Ephesians 5:32), a holy mystery or sacrament which reflects the covenant union of the faithful love between Christ and the Church, and which itself becomes a channel of love and grace in the world. For each human being to make such a covenant is for him or her to realize an important part of what it means to be made in God's image. It means to further his primary and ultimate purpose in creation by reproducing the kind of creative (but not necessarily procreative) self-giving love that is basic to God's own nature. Accepting homosexual relationships does not mean jettisoning this fundamental biblical teaching about the sacramental character of human sexuality.

Those who continue to cling to a natural law argument against homosexuality on the basis of Romans 1 should also be reminded that Paul appeals more frequently and clearly to natural law and the creation story in order to justify his now abandoned teachings about the veiling and silencing of women. Paul said that women must be veiled because man was created first and it is primarily man who is the image of God (1 Corinthians 11:7–8). It is shameful for a man to wear long hair and a woman to wear short hair because 'nature itself teaches us so' (1 Corinthians 11:14; a much clearer expression of 'natural law' than anything in Romans 1). No woman is permitted to teach or to hold authority over men, and women are commanded to be silent 'because Adam was formed first, then Eve; and Adam was not deceived, but the woman was deceived and became a transgressor' (1 Timothy 2:12–14). These are theological arguments which appeal to God's plan in creation no less than Romans 1:18ff., and indeed Paul is much clearer about their authoritative status and the practical rules he intends to deduce from them, even to the point of saying the silencing of women is a command of the Lord, and if anyone disputes it he is to be rejected (1 Corinthians 14:33–8). It is obvious that Paul lays far more weight of doctrine and authority on this teaching about women than on his passing references to homosexuality. Yet the fact that today it is consistently ignored, even in the most traditional churches, is not felt to 'deny the doctrine of creation' or 'to alter fundamentally the whole biblical teaching on creation, sex, marriage, forgiveness and redemption'.

I remarked that the original biblical prohibition of homosexuality was probably written in the situation of the Babylonian exile, as a mark of Jewish separateness from the surrounding culture. Babylon remains a powerful symbol for modern secular society, and in one sense it might fairly be argued that the situation of Christians has *not* changed. As 'aliens and exiles' Christians still understand themselves to be called, no less than the Jews in Babylon, to a distinctive morality and a distinctive holiness which will challenge the world in sexual matters as in all else (1 Peter 2:3). This is not to be denied. The point is that the most distinctive and constructive witness that homosexual Christians can offer, both to 'Babylon' in the shape of the secular gay scene and to the Church itself, is the witness of relationships marked by the same quality of holy and faithful love to which heterosexual Christians are called in marriage.

Is It Moral?

More Natural Law

If the person in the street objects to homosexual practice, the chances are that the objection will be based first of all on a common-sense form of the natural law argument similar to Paul's in Romans 1. Homosexuality does not seem to fit the observed order of nature. There are, after all, two sexes. (To borrow a famous *bon mot* of Anita Bryant, God made Adam and Eve, not Adam and Steve.) There is also an argument from design. Our genital equipment exists primarily for procreation, and in gay sex procreation is not a possibility. More fundamentally, two male or two female bodies simply do not fit together in the same way as a male and a female. In particular some objectors have a very strong instinctive reaction against the 'unnaturalness' of anal sex – though of course this is not the only, or even the predominant, form of homosexual activity, and like all forms of homosexual activity, it also occurs among heterosexuals.

Some statements of the natural law argument are plainly wrong. One of the oldest is in Plato (though he himself did not hold to it): that because homosexual activity does not occur among animals, it ought not to be done among humans either. Here in fact the basic premise is simply mistaken: homosexual activity is common to many classes of animals, and in this sense is therefore perfectly 'natural'. But there is a more important consideration that tells against the natural law argument in general. The truth is that in other matters we do not regulate our behaviour or derive our moral precepts simply from observation of what nature does or does not do. Civilization itself depends on our disobeying many instincts and urges which might be termed 'natural'. We are constantly re-inventing, adapting, manipulating and often reversing the ways of the natural world in order to serve what seems to us a higher good, a better 'law'. At this level the natural law argument against homosexuality has as much force as the early objection to aviation on the grounds that 'if God had meant us to fly he'd have given us wings'.

More specifically, in managing nature we do not usually have qualms about adapting, altering or reversing natural bodily processes and functions in order to prolong or enhance life. Medicine and surgery are obvious examples. We intervene to maximize the capacities of our bodies and the health and wholeness of our lives. Even if one were to accept the demeaning view of homosexuality as a disorder or handicap, we do not condemn the 'handicapped' for adapting and using in the best and most creative way possible the gifts and capacities which they possess. One rather applauds and supports them. Those who claim to be repelled and disgusted by homosexual forms of intercourse might ask why they are not disgusted by a painter who expresses his creativity by painting with his feet; or by an author who types by blowing down a tube. (They should also, of course, ask themselves whether they object to similar sexual acts between heterosexuals, and if not, why not). I would reject the term 'handicap' for homosexuality (except in so far as gay people are handicapped by other people's prejudices), but I believe there is a true analogy between the homosexual's so-called 'unnatural' use of his or her physical equipment to make love and these examples of the 'unnatural' use of the body to make art.

It is worth noting here that the long and unresolved 'nature versus nurture' debate as to the cause of homosexuality has no proper bearing on discussion of the morality of homosexual practice. Campaigners for the acceptance of gay relationships have tended to insist on a genetic origin, on the grounds that it would seem to confirm that homosexuality is a 'given' of creation, and therefore 'natural' and willed by God. Thinking along the same lines of a false natural law argument, opponents have tended to see it as a psychological disorder, due to parental or other 'mistakes', and therefore attributable to human failure and not to the will of God. However, even if the origin of homosexuality could be shown to be genetic or psychological (and it is just as likely to be both), that would not tell us whether the phenomenon of homosexuality is good or bad, willed by God or not. Genetic conditioning produces good things and bad things, things like the wonderful diversity of races and features and capacities, which we believe is part of God's will in creation, and things like congenital disease, which we believe is not. Equally our psychological conditioning can work for good or ill. What matters morally for all of us is not so much how we come to be what we are, but what we do with it.

The Purpose of Sex

Homosexual activity of course does not fit the natural pattern of procreation. But we are long past arguing – unless we are extremely conservative Roman Catholics – that sexual activity is only right and good when there is a possibility of childbirth. It is true that Anglican bishops argued against contraception on these grounds in 1930, but we can safely say that the position has now been abandoned. In any case, the idea that procreation was a necessary condition for moral sexual union was never logically or rigorously applied. Even the most conservative Churches have generally accepted that sexual relations are permissible within marriages where one or both partners are infertile, or past the age of childbearing. This is clearly because within such a marriage sexual activity has always been perceived as good in itself, quite apart from any possibility of childbirth.

If we ask what are the legitimating purposes of sex in marriage, the *Book of Common Prayer* laid down three. First, the procreation of children. Second, 'a remedy against sin, and to avoid fornication'. Third, 'for the mutual society help and comfort that the one ought to have of the other, both in prosperity and in adversity'. *The Alternative Service Book* puts the same thing rather more positively (and puts procreation last). Marriage is:

> a gift of God in creation and a means of his grace, a holy mystery in which a man and woman become one flesh. It is God's purpose that, as husband and wife give themselves to one another in love throughout their lives, they shall be united in that love as Christ is united with his Church.

> Marriage is given that husband and wife may comfort and help each other, living faithfully together in need and plenty, in sorrow and in joy. It is given, that with delight and tenderness they may know each other in love, and through the joy of their bodily union, may strengthen the union of their hearts and lives. It is given that they may have children and be blessed in caring for them and bringing them up in accordance with God's will, to his praise and glory.

With the exception of childbirth all these purposes of marriage can be fulfilled in a permanent, faithful, stable gay relationship, and are being fulfilled in many. The case of an infertile heterosexual couple proves that the absence of the possibility of procreation cannot mean that the attempt to achieve these other purposes of God in creating sexual love thereby becomes immoral. The onus is therefore on those who reject homosexual relationships to show where the difference lies in moral status between an infertile marriage and a committed gay relationship. I do not believe that such a difference can in fact be shown.

Moral or Social Status?

At this point the person in the street may balk again. How can one claim that a gay or lesbian relationship is equivalent in status to a marriage? Professors of moral theology may balk too. In a letter I received from one of these, he declined to contribute to a projected book on the subject of homosexual monogamy. He explained that although he sympathized with the position I am putting forward here, he felt unable sincerely to defend an *equivalence* between Christian marriage and a committed gay relationship,

---

knowing that he would still prefer his own children or grandchildren to be married than to take a same-sex partner.

Unfortunately the professor did not explain whether his preference was based on theology or instinct, but I strongly suspect the latter. In the first place, I have to be clear (and should have made it clearer to the professor) that I am of course talking about an equivalence of Christian moral status or acceptability between marriage and gay partnership, not an equivalence of current social or personal desirability. If I had children, I expect I too would prefer them to marry, in the first place because I too would hope for grandchildren, and in the second place, because I would not wish on anyone who could avoid it the massive strain which is imposed on gay relationships from outside. The inability to bear their own children (I mean the inability to bear children together, of course, in the case of lesbians) and the difficulty of adopting is a real cause of sadness for same-sex couples, as it is for heterosexual couples who cannot have children. Equally the difficulty of sustaining a permanent, faithful, stable gay relationship in the present climate of Church and society is not to be underestimated (though seeing this should drive us to change, not accept the prejudices that make it so). For these reasons I accept that at the practical level, a gay relationship is disadvantaged as against a marriage.

But to be socially disadvantaged is not the same as to be wrong or morally inferior. Even if childbearing marriage is seen as the 'best' in terms of its relative chance of practical and personal fulfilment, that does not make it the enemy of the good in the case of those for whom the 'best' is not an option. On the contrary, as even the bishops' Statement recognizes, even in such adverse circumstances there are homosexual couples

> who grow steadily in fidelity and in mutual caring, understanding and support, whose partnerships are a blessing to the world around them, and who achieve great, even heroic sacrifice and devotion.

It is good to reach such an affirmation, but it must be said that there is an odd disjunction between, on the one hand, this observation and the positive tone of the first four chapters of the Statement, and on the other the conclusions drawn in the fifth chapter. It is extraordinary that the Statement in its first section appears to accept the objections to the traditional arguments against homosexual practice which I have outlined, yet at the end simply restates the natural law argument in its crudest form:

> Homophile orientation and its expression in sexual activity do not constitute a parallel and alternative form of human sexuality as complete within the created order as the heterosexual ... heterosexuality and homosexuality are not equally congruous with the observed order of creation ...

In the same section a homosexual relationship is also said to be less 'valid' and 'not on a par with heterosexual marriage as a reflection of God's purposes in creation'.

But if a homosexual relationship can be 'a blessing to the world around', and 'a way of heroic self-sacrifice and devotion', in what precise sense is it 'less valid' and 'unequal'? Apparently not in a moral sense, since the bishops accept that a homosexual relationship can carry these marks of holiness, and that it is the most constructive and positive thing that some individuals can do with their own nature. The bishops are also at pains to point out that homosexuals are not to be devalued as people, and that to categorize homosexuality as a sickness to be healed is inappropriate, dangerous and degrading. So what kind of inferiority is left? Once these possibilities are excluded, the statement that homosexuality is not 'congruous with the observed order of creation', seems to amount to no more than the trivial observation that it is a minority orientation and does not produce children. (One might point out that celibacy is equally a minority orientation which does not produce children, and equally incongruous with the observed order of nature, though for most of its history the Church has tended to regard it as more valid than and indeed superior to marriage.)

It is hard to avoid the conclusion that the natural law objection has simply been re-imported at the end of the bishops' Statement, just at the point where practical action has to be broached, in order to express what is really no more than my professor's, and my own, undeniable and instinctive feeling that a homosexual relationship is less 'complete' (I accept the bishops' word) because it cannot bear children, and less convenient because of social custom and other people's prejudice. If more than this is intended it needs clarifying, because I have not been able to find any other reason for this 'inequality' or 'lesser validity' in the report. Again I would focus on the question: does it imply any moral or religious or personal difference (i.e. any difference which is not the obvious physical one) between a committed gay relationship and an infertile marriage? If so, what is it?

Complementarity

One possible response might be to suggest that as well as having bodies which are designed to fit together in a particular way, the two sexes are also meant to fit together emotionally and mentally. So it is sometimes argued that homosexual relationships are wrong, and perhaps more likely to fail, because they lack the element of a psychological complementarity which is supposedly an important feature of heterosexual relationships.

It seems to be scientifically provable that *in general* there are real differences between the psychology of the two sexes. There is even some recent scientific evidence that they are traceable to different configurations in the male and female brain. The stereotypes are well known. Men are supposedly active, dominant, individualistic, aggressive and analytical, valuing theoretical thought and perception. Women are supposedly passive, social, bonding and nurturing, valuing instinctual thought and emotional perception ... and so on. There may be a certain practical value in perceiving these differences as collective generalizations, but we have rightly learned to be wary of them because we have seen that injustice and oppression invariably come in when these generalizations are imposed on individuals as normative rules. The feminist movement is a reaction against precisely this kind of oppression, and recent phenomena like the 'new man' concept or Robert Bly's 'wildman' movement are equally a reaction against the imposition of 'macho' images and norms of behaviour on men. For this reason, in secular relationships, as in current pastoral theology, the emphasis has moved sharply from the distinction of gender norms to the equality of human persons, and so to an open and interchangeable complementarity of roles. Few Christians would now criticize a marriage in which, say, the wife was the principal earner and the husband stayed at home as nurturer. On the contrary, we might praise the couple's adaptability. Having reached this understanding, it would be highly unreasonable to continue to argue against a homosexual relationship on the grounds of a supposed incompatibility of stereotypes, when we no longer recognize those stereotypes as normative in marriage.

In fact, just as rigid stereotypes of masculinity and femininity are breaking down in marriage, it seems they are breaking down in homosexual partnerships too. Whereas in the past homosexuals typically adopted an active or passive role on the traditional model of marriage, Terry Sanderson, in a (mostly) admirable book called *Making Gay Relationships Work*, writes:

> Research – and our own observations – have proved that the 'butch-femme' scenario of gay relationships is rare these days, if not altogether extinct . . . We are far more likely to base our relationships on the 'best friend' model, a far superior arrangement that produces an egalitarian framework within which to function. This has

advantages over the traditional heterosexual model which frequently reduces the woman to the status of subordinate ... How many married women wish they could be best friends with their husband instead of being his drudge and servant?

An American psychological counsellor, writing a similar book for lesbians and gay men, also notes with approval that male-female role distinctions now tend to characterize only the relationships of more elderly lesbians. She advises – as any good marriage counsellor might – that even if a 'leader' role is more natural to one partner, and a more passive role to the other, the essential thing is not to make the roles mutually exclusive or irreversible, and never to take the other for granted (T. Tessina).

It is obvious that any couple, homosexual or heterosexual, must find a way of living together which accords with their own instincts and temperament (gender-conditioned or otherwise) and which allows each of them a fair share of freedom and responsibility. For any couple this is a large part of learning to love and grow together. In a fine and moving passage of the Statement the bishops say of marriage:

> A true marriage reflects Christ's own love for us all. He too gave himself to others 'for better for worse, till death'. In it we learn to break down our pride and self-concern, to be open to our partner as he or she really is, to treasure what is good, and forgive faults, to sacrifice ourselves for the sake of the other, to be loyal whatever the price. ... A good marriage creates for each partner the same kind of environment which we recognize as promoting growth to maturity in the case of children: a

combination of love and challenge within an unbreakably reliable relationship.

Precisely the same is true of a gay relationship. In fact it is striking to read how closely the bishops' portrait of a good marriage resembles the secular recipe of Tessina and Sanderson for successful gay and lesbian partnerships – though they might all be very surprised to realize it!

Friendship or Monogamy?

I have just quoted with approval the statement that in gay relationships the model of partnership is more often that of the best friend than that of marriage in the traditional heterosexual mould. But I believe it is a serious mistake, leading to serious moral consequences, to use the term 'friendship' as the primary term for a same-sex relationship. Of course it is true of both a heterosexual marriage and a committed gay partnership that the most successful relationship is likely to be one in which the couple are best friends as well as sexual partners. But in Christian doctrine a marriage, even considered apart from procreation, is far more than friendship, and the term friendship is wholly inadequate to cover what marriage and sexual commitment imply theologically. Friendship in any normal use of the term does not imply sexual activity, still less in any theological use, and it is an abuse to try to force it to do so. One may have many friends; one may not, within any moral framework which remotely links with Christian teaching, have many sexual partners.

My rejection of the term 'friendship' as the appro-priate term for any sexually-expressed partnership is diametrically opposed to the views of the two best-known Christian gay writers in Britain in recent years, Elizabeth Stuart and Michael Vasey. Vasey's book *Friends and Strangers* is a plea, written from the perspective of a gay Evangelical, for the inclusion of the gay Christian experience within the Church. His analysis of the biblical material relating to the issue is especially compelling and perceptive. Vasey does not attempt, however, to build a theological model for gay relationships or offer any moral framework for homosexual practice. Rather, by repeatedly asserting that 'there are no blueprints' for gay relationships, and viewing them in contradistinction to heterosexual marriage, he effectively cuts gay people off from any positive theological self-understanding or moral guidance which the Christian tradition might offer. This leaves him apparently pleading for the Church to accept gay relationships on any terms whatever.

Elizabeth Stuart in her books *Daring to Speak Love's Name* and *Just Good Friends* sets out to to develop a 'lesbian and gay theology of relationships' based entirely on the category of friendship. She insists most emphatically (and in this agrees with the bishops' Statement) that lesbian and gay relationships are not marriages, and that blessings of these relationships are not weddings. Her rejection of the terms 'marriage' and 'monogamy' as descriptions of gay relationships derives from her unwillingness to accept that marriage or monogamy can be isolated from 'patriarchal' domination and abuse. On similar grounds she refuses any application of covenant theology to sexual relationships, regarding the prophets' description of the marriage between Yahweh and Israel, or the Pauline description of marriage as the 'mystery' of Christ and the Church, as being inextricably tied to assumptions of slavery and subjugation. In the later book she effectively rejects marriage itself as being inherently a tool of patriarchal control. Any attempt to gain acceptance of gay relationships on similar terms is therefore essentially misguided:

> What is the ultimate value of incorporation into an institution which even heterosexuals are asking serious questions about, an institution which was born, formed and structured for and by patriarchy? (*Just Good Friends*, p. 174)

Stuart admits that there may be some happy marriages, but only as it were by accident, when married people strive to 'subvert' the institution into something which it inherently is not.

Here is a gulf, probably unbridgeable, between Stuart's view and mine. Unlike Stuart, I do not despair of monogamy, and continue to understand marriage as a gift of God and a sacrament of the Church. I do not accept that it is essentially and irredeemably patriarchal, even though it is undeniably bound up with patriarchy and male 'headship' in its origins and development. For all the criticism that can fairly be levelled at marriage as practised through history and in the present, inequality and injustice are not a necessary part of the institution, as many if not most contemporary marriages show. No one could deny the evils and injustices which marriage has meant for many, and especially for women. But *abusus non tollit usum* – abuse does not argue for disuse; and *corruptio optimi pessima* – it is the corruption of the best which is the worst. A genuinely equal, happy and mutually affirming marriage is not such a rare phenomenon – and monogamy is still the framework within which the great majority of women and men choose to live their lives. Seen in this perspective Stuart's attitude of total rejection, while it may be understandable from a particular lesbian and feminist standpoint, looks quite unreasonably negative and pessimistic.

This difference of view is really the central issue for Christian sexual ethics today, far more crucial than the 'gay issue' alone. It is a fundamental question about human nature, about the way we are made and the way we can expect to find fulfilment. Is it true that the capacity to make a covenant of lifelong, committed, faithful love with one person is one of God's greatest gifts, a reflection in us of his own nature? Is it true that for most people it is the best framework for personal flourishing, the best in which *both* partners can grow to be *more* freely and fully themselves? Or is believing and attempting this no more than what Stuart calls 'the idolatry of the ideal', setting up a prison which in practice almost inevitably generates misery, guilt and abuse? Closely tied to this question is a second. How does the context of sexual activity relate to the wellbeing of the human person? Is it best if sexual intercourse happens only within, and as an expression of, this kind of personal covenant? Or is sexual intercourse detachable from commitment, and the context in which it occurs a matter of moral and spiritual indifference?

In Stuart's view:

There would seem to be nothing inherently wrong with friends who are not involved in relationships of radical vulnerability (i.e. of personal commitment) enjoying intimate physical relations, as long as these are negotiated honestly with all concerned. If we accept, as we surely must, that acts of physical intimacy have no inherent meaning, then the onus is on the friends to establish the boundaries of their relationship. (*Just Good Friends*, p. 224)

The most startling part of this statement is the throwaway line, 'If we accept, as we surely must, that acts of physical intimacy have no inherent meaning ...'. In Stuart's view, the meaning or meaninglessness of sexual activity entirely depends on context. She believes that, because 'there is no universal meaning to sex ... and genital contact is not "the ultimate" expression of closeness', then even anonymously promiscuous sex may be 'unproblematic'. The only moral criteria for sexual activity, even between total strangers, are consent, honesty and non-exploitation. I will say more about gay promiscuity in the next chapter. But it is worth observing here that for an author who accuses the Church of dualism – that is, an unhealthy separation of body and soul – it is a remarkable assumption that what one does with one's body sexually can be regarded as detachable from and irrelevant to one's person.

Stuart claims to be offering an 'empirical theology', one based on her own knowledge of the secular gay subculture. But Christian theology is about more than describing 'what happens': it is an attempt to understand – and ultimately to redeem – 'what happens' in relation to profound truths about human nature revealed in Scripture and Christian tradition. The best Stuart can do in this respect is to try and find paradigms in Scripture and tradition for her model of sexually expressed friendship. Although she admits at one point that one cannot prove that any of these friendships involved sexual expression, she nevertheless repeatedly refers to David and Jonathan, Ruth and Naomi, Jesus and the beloved disciple, as if it *were* proved that they were sexually expressed. Similarly she calls on Aelred of Rievaulx in support, but Aelred, who was almost certainly homosexual himself, was perfectly clear that, though limited physical demonstrations of affection between particular monastic friends could be countenanced, sex could not – for the very practical reason that it would create division and destruction in the community. We know from Aelred's own writings that Stuart's notion of open sexual friendship was abhorrent to him, not simply because (as she believes) he had 'internalized the fears of his age', but more importantly because he knew from experience that *it does not work*: uncovenanted sex generates envy and instability, which in turn make community relationships impossible.

For similar reasons, although Stuart is right in accusing me of giving primacy to Scripture and tradition, I believe my own views are no less empirically and practically based than hers. Observation of 'what happens', both on the 'gay scene' and on the 'straight scene', leads me to believe very strongly that the Church's wisdom in advising men and women to confine sexual activity to permanent, faithful relationships remains as wise as it ever was. On the firmly empirical basis of having picked up the pieces of too many damaged people, I am convinced that anonymous or 'recreational' sex is *never* 'unproblematic' or irrelevant to a person's emotional and spiritual health. On the contrary, quite apart from the guilt and fear which are usually involved, like other addictions it dulls the appetite for normal life, and creates a peculiar kind of introversion, a sense of inner exile which is ultimately destructive of real relationships. Paul's statement that sexual activity divorced from loving commitment 'tears away' part of the person, whether one wills it or not, is a matter of experience, not theological theory. The same holds true of sexually 'open' relationships. Honesty is a necessary, but hardly a sufficient condition for a happy relationship, and in practice sexual envy and competition, fear of disease, fear of ageing, the cult of youth, the sense of being robbed of a partner's emotional and sexual energy, and above all the emotional insecurity of constantly wondering how much one is loved and for what and for how long – all contribute to instability and likely destruction.

Michael Vasey's insistence that there are 'no blueprints' for gay relationships, and Elizabeth Stuart's rejection of monogamy and endorsement of sexually open 'friendships', for all their Christian packaging, derive from an uncritical acceptance of the tenets of secular sexual liberationism. They give no clue as to what a distinctively Christian homosexual relationship might be. They offer no engagement with the deep mainstream of Christian teaching about the sacredness of sex or the importance of sexual discipline for personal integrity, and they leave gay people with no moral structure or guiding wisdom for building emotionally secure and sexually healthy lives. Their views, translated into behaviour, are physically as well as spiritually dangerous; Michael himself died of AIDS in 1999. It is worth pondering this judgement by Andrew Sullivan, whose own arguments for covenant monogamy are conditioned by his own close empirical knowledge of the American gay scene over the last ten years. He too is HIV positive.

> The gay liberationists have plenty to answer for. For far too long they promoted the tragic lie that no avenue of sexuality was any better or nobler than any other; that all demands for responsibility or fidelity or commitment or even healthier psychological integration were mere covers for 'neoconservatism' or worse, 'self-hatred'; that even in the teeth of a viral catastrophe, saving lives was less important than saving a culture of 'promiscuity as a collective way of life', when, of course, it was little more than a collective way of death. They have demeaned gay men almost as surely as their unwitting allies, the fundamentalists. (*Love Undetectable*, p. 52)

Is It Achievable?

Promiscuity and Fidelity

Two courageous London priests pioneered blessing ceremonies for homosexual couples through the 1980s. Though they have now been joined by many more, these two have probably officiated at more such ceremonies than any others in the country, by this time numbering some hundreds. They testify that they have always offered couples the choice of making temporary vows, or vows, as in marriage, of permanent, lifelong faithfulness. Both report that all but a tiny number have chosen to make lifelong vows to one another. As far as these priests can tell, the success rate of these couples in terms of durability is high – certainly not lower than that of the 'normal' marriages which they have also celebrated week by week.

Evidence of this kind and the increasing visibility of long-term gay relationships today makes it virtually impossible to repeat the old prejudice that 'they can't last'. They obviously can and do. It is a testimony to the reality and strength of the monogamous instinct in all human beings that gay relationships succeed despite the lack of any legal framework or social support, despite the absence of the cohesive force of childrearing, and despite the constant undermining force of ecclesiastical and social hostility. When one remembers that even with all the support which Church and society supply the success rate of heterosexual monogamy is not impressive, the fact that so many gay relationships achieve permanence may seem little short of miraculous.

There is no reason to believe that homosexual men are naturally more inclined to promiscuity than heterosexual men. At the level of biological instinct, probably both are equally strongly inclined to the purely mechanical release of sexual energy – more strongly in general than women, for whom sexual activity is widely agreed to be less driven and immediate in kind, and more dependent on personal and relational conditions. However, there are at least two special factors which may make homosexual men statistically more promiscuous than heterosexuals. The first is that in the absence of opportunities in ordinary life for meeting other gay people, and without accepted social structures within which 'courting' can take place, homosexual couples tend to move more rapidly to sexual expression than heterosexual couples. The second factor is the comparative availability of promiscuous sex. For a heterosexual man, finding a woman to have sex with is likely to be a time-consuming and expensive activity. For homosexual men, at least in an urban area, finding another man for the impersonal, rapid release of sexual energy is likely to be an easy matter, however dangerous and demeaning it may be. For some it becomes a compulsive addiction.

The phenomenon of promiscuous homosexual activity bolsters hostile feelings in society towards homosexuals in general. In matters of prejudice fine distinctions are not made: gay people are seen as those 'who do that kind of thing'. To some extent this negative, marginalizing attitude may also be internalized by gay people themselves, who find themselves living up – or down – to precisely the expectations society has of them. It is particularly unfortunate and unfair that whereas most stable homosexual relationships are still secret and invisible to society, so that this 'model' is rarely seen, promiscuous homosexual behaviour or behaviour involving minors is frequently prosecuted and reported in the media, and so readily becomes associated in the public mind with homosexuality in general. Homosexuals are readily assumed to be promiscuous or paedophile because only promiscuous or paedophile homosexuals get to be known about.

It is worth noting that this particular catch-22 can also affect bishops. Bishops who are known to have negative views about homosexuality naturally do not receive the confidences of their gay clergy, and are likely to remain unaware of their existence. The only gay clergy they get to know about are the ones who get into trouble. They are then prone to view all gay people in the same light – which bolsters the negative views they held in the first place. I have met two or three bishops whose thinking was very clearly conditioned in this way by having to deal with errant clergy. Several bishops seem quite unaware of the numbers of gay clergy in their dioceses who live in good, sustaining and faithful gay partnerships. One or two have even announced that they have no practising gay clergy in their diocese at all, to the grim amusement of the 'non-existent' clergy in question!

Statistics about promiscuous sexual activity are revealing. Police reports show that approximately half of those arrested for homosexual activity in public places are married men, and we can reasonably take this to be an accurate sample of the whole. This little-known fact seems to me enormously significant. It suggests that a large number of men who are predominantly or at least significantly homosexual in orientation, having adopted for whatever reason the course of marriage, are driven to seek satisfaction for their true sexual nature in this way. It is fair to ask how many of them would have been saved from the misery of their situation if building a decent same-sex partnership had ever been presented to them as a viable option.

Two more sets of statistics, taken from surveys of the behaviour of gay men in the USA and in France, demonstrate that the incidence of promiscuous activity among gay men falls dramatically when they enter into a stable relationship. This is proof positive that gay monogamy, no less than marriage, fulfils its Prayer Book function as a 'remedy against sin'. Again it is fair to ask how many gay men would have been saved from the degradation of promiscuous and compulsive sex if they had had the chance of living and loving in a stable relationship.

Nevertheless, a serious temptation remains for homosexuals in a committed partnership, as well as for single or celibate or married homosexuals, who remain aware of the easy availability of casual sex on the gay scene. Someone in this situation is not helped by the relatively light view taken of casual sex in much of the gay subculture, and even in some Christian gay publications such as those criticized in the last chapter. It is true, of course, that far more is involved in the concept of faithfulness to another person than sexual fidelity alone. It is also true that sexual sin is not the worst sin, and that an act of sexual infidelity need not mean the destruction of a relationship. But we need to counter the idea that promiscuous gay sex is somehow more excusable than promiscuous heterosexual sex, or that it is a morally irrelevant expression of biological need ('little more than sneezing', as I once heard it described). Nor will it do to suggest that a Christian sexual relationship or a Christian liturgy of commitment may or may not involve vows of sexual fidelity, or to imply that a sexually open relationship can be as valid as a sexually exclusive one.

This is not merely a matter of rules but of personal and spiritual realities. As has already been observed, at the practical level, within a heterosexual marriage or a homosexual partnership, couples who begin by allowing sexual openness regularly find that it ends in jealousy, hurt and destruction. Christians above all cannot lose sight of the fact that sex is not to be isolated from the totality of who and what we are. Jack Dominian, who has written powerfully about the relationship between sex and personal integrity, strongly advocates that the Church should do all it can to encourage faithful relationships among homosexuals as a way to integration and spiritual maturity. He observes that there is psychological as well as theological truth in Paul's observation that sex always has spiritual consequences for the person, whether for good or ill. Sex has its own dynamic; it always tends to give life and 'make love', but where it is torn away from all possibility of love in personal commitment it tends instead ultimately to futility, desecration, the dis-integration of the person.

Jim Cotter in an essay on 'The Shaping of Gay Relationships' remarks, quoting Harry Williams on chastity:

> It is precisely because sex is so powerful a desire that it can make a takeover bid and dominate our lives. It is precisely because the person may be highly sexed and know the power of the junkie and the prostitute within that the quality of the relationship with the other needs to be kept central ... 'Emotional chastity consists of the attempt to discover our own genuine deep feelings and of being loyal to them even when temporary feelings of an opposite but more superficial kind bang noisily within us.' We may have to discern in life not only what is the lesser of two evils, but also what is the greater of two goods. And that will involve times of saying No for the sake of times of saying Yes.

As I said at the start, we all inhabit glass houses, and there are times when we all fail and need forgiveness, if only in the matter of 'looking lustfully'. To recognize this and to treat it compassionately is not the same as to abandon Christian ethics and pretend that chastity, in the true sense of sexual fidelity and integrity, does not matter. It does matter, and within the conditions of the secular gay scene it is specially important for gay Christians to witness to it.

Being Exemplary: Clergy in Homosexual Relationships

We have, therefore, to say that in our considered judgment the clergy cannot claim the liberty to enter into sexually active homophile relationships. Because of the distinctive nature of their calling, status and consecration, to allow such a claim on their part would be seen as placing that way of life in all respects on a par with heterosexual marriage as the reflection of God's purposes in creation. The church cannot accept such a parity and remain faithful to the insights which God has given through scripture, tradition and reasoned reflection on experience.

This is the conclusion of the bishops' Statement on the question of homosexual relationships and the clergy. Earlier I focused on the crucial issue as to what the bishops mean by this 'imparity' between homosexual and heterosexual relationships, and why this is seen as a deciding factor in respect of the clergy's 'exemplary' function. The bishops earlier in the report make it clear that they do not consider a faithful homosexual relationship a vicious or morally inferior way of life; otherwise they could not recommend the acceptance of such relationships into congregations, nor say that such couples can be a 'blessing to the world around them, and . . . achieve great, even heroic sacrifice and devotion'. The 'imparity' cannot reside in the impossibility of childbirth, since there is no bar on clergy in infertile marriages. Even if the bishops regard homosexuality as a handicap, there is no bar on handicapped clergy. Nor are celibate clergy debarred in the Anglican Church, despite the fact that such a state arguably flies more directly in the face of 'God's purposes declared in creation'. So why, having concluded after a reasoned reassessment of Scripture, tradition and experience, that for lay homosexuals a faithful, stable, permanent relationship may be God's call and their way to holiness, do the bishops say this cannot be so among the clergy?

The ruling is linked to the statement that clergy are called to exemplify an ideal, but that (in this mysterious and unspecified way) clergy in a homosexual partnership fall short of the ideal and therefore cannot be a good example. Of course for most heterosexuals faithful marriage is the ideal – and there are faithful married clergy to exemplify it. For those who are called to celibacy, clergy or laypeople, faithful celibacy is the ideal, and there are faithful celibate clergy to exemplify it. I have argued that for homosexuals who are not called to celibacy faithful monogamous partnership is the ideal (and in the case of lay people the bishops seem to accept it) – and there are in fact faithful clergy partnerships to exemplify it too. But this, the bishops say, is wrong.

The position is the more ironic because if there is a single group of people who desperately need an ideal and role-models to exemplify it, it is gay people. Frankly, it seems a doubtful proposition that many heterosexual parishioners look to the local vicar and his wife as their icon of married bliss. It seems unlikely too that very many model themselves on clergy in following a celibate life. On the other hand, it is the experience of many clergy in gay relationships who have allowed this to be known, that they rapidly draw a large clientele of other gay people who cannot find the kind of positive Christian counselling they need anywhere else. In this situation, more than any other I know, the role-model of the priest really is indispensable, and becomes a rock on which others can build.

But it is intolerably hard for clergy to fill this need if their own support from the Church is withdrawn.

The bishops' conclusion is dismaying for another reason. Many of the bishops who acquiesced in it know perfectly well, and in private fully accept, that some of their clergy are in gay relationships. There are many clergy in the Church who have insisted on being honest about their private lives with their ordaining and employing bishops, with those who selected them for training, with their training college principals, and with others in authority. It is extraordinary that so many bishops under the cloak of collective anonymity have allowed this private support to be publicly withdrawn, presumably for the sake of political pragmatism. In the aftermath of the Statement's publication a number of bishops contacted their gay clergy to assure them that it didn't really mean what it said. That was kind, but hardly admirable.

In the Preface to the Statement it is underlined that it is a transitional document, intended to promote an educational process. Yet the bishops themselves must realize that no effective process of education will begin in the Church until they see to it that 'what is whispered in private rooms is shouted from the housetops'. This means taking their episcopal teaching office seriously, and finding the courage to let even 'difficult' conservative Evangelicals know their real views. The gospel does not allow a divergence between public and private moralities, and political expediency is not a Christian virtue – rather the opposite. The unity of the Church should not be bought at the price of hypocrisy, or of scapegoating those who are seldom in a position to defend themselves. If, as all the private evidence shows, the majority of bishops in the Church are in fact willing to accept and support their gay clergy, they should be prepared to stand up themselves and teach their people why. They may even find – as many gay clergy have found – that by doing so respect is won and opposition melts away.

Dr Ben Fletcher, in a survey of stress among the clergy, wrote in conclusion, with gay clergy particularly in view:

> It is surely now necessary for the Church to change policy. Evidence shows that committed relationships provide partners with a protective buffer against stress and illness. . . . What is needed surely is a positive ethic for committed and stable homosexual relationships analogous to heterosexual marriage. The Church needs to encourage a lifelong commitment between homosexual partners in much the same way it does between heterosexual partners.

Liturgies, Recognition and Acceptance

Nevertheless, it would be foolish to underestimate the strength of fear and prejudice which still surrounds homosexuality. Things are changing, but still in our society and in our Church injustices, insults and vilification are regularly heaped on gay people which would be illegal if perpetrated against other minority groups. If the bishops are serious about healing this prejudice and urging congregations to welcome and support homosexuals, they could take no more positive steps themselves than to permit the official use of a liturgy to ratify the vows and bless the union of a same-sex couple. If, as the bishops have affirmed, a faithful gay relationship can be a 'source of blessing' to the partners and to others around them, what warrant is there for refusing to give it the blessing of the Church?

A number of such liturgies have been printed, and are used unofficially with increasing frequency. For the reasons I have already discussed I believe that any liturgy which is used to ratify and bless a sexual relationship ought to be undergirded by a strong sacramental theology of sex, and for that reason I do not think the Church could approve the use of such a service, any more than it could provide a form of marriage, unless it rested on similar vows of permanence, fidelity, and stability. It is extremely encouraging to know that gay people who approach the Church for blessings almost invariably want their relationship to rest on vows of this kind.

It is important to remember, of course, that the Church does not marry anyone. The Anglican understanding of marriage is that the couple themselves are the ministers of the sacrament. The Church hears and approves the promises which the partners make to one another, and adds its blessing to their commitment. By doing so it also implies its willingness to support in every practical and spiritual way possible the keeping of that commitment. Every mature married couple knows, and the bishops emphasize in their Statement, that a successful marriage cannot and must not be a private, inward-looking arrangement – 'selfishness for two' – but depends on a whole network of supporting relationships with those around. The marriage service itself asks God to give the couple grace to minister to others, and to be a witness to Christ's saving love in the world: 'It is the strength of this many-dimensioned partnership which will make them a more effective means of grace together than they would have been apart.'

An officially endorsed liturgy of blessing, as well as affirming God's love for the couple themselves, would help immeasurably towards creating in society the same acceptance and support for gay partnerships that any marriage needs to flourish. Among the sadnesses frequently imposed on gay people are the inability to celebrate their relationship publicly and the need to keep their love secret from family or colleagues or friends. As Sanderson notes in *Making Gay Relationships Work*, this enforced secrecy robs the relationship of dignity, denies it space to grow, and deprives it of the kind of support network that we recognize is essential to a marriage. Maximizing the possibility of openness and sharing is as vital to the health of a gay relationship as to any other. Heterosexual Christians of goodwill need to recognize the heroic level of courage and the cost which may be involved in overcoming the fear of 'coming out'. If they are in a position to help, there is plenty of help they can give. For homosexual partnerships simple things that married couples take for granted – joint invitations, anniversary cards, inquiries about one's partner – become immensely important signs of affirmation. The whole point is that, whatever one calls it, the relationship is analogous to a marriage, and should be reacted to in the same way. There will be no reality behind the bishops urging the acceptance of homosexual couples by churches unless this is taken on board.

One of the most curious arguments against recognizing gay partnerships is that it would constitute a threat to 'family values' or to the social order at large. Yet the point of my argument is that, at both the theological and the social level, the acceptance of same-sex partners in covenant relationships does not overturn the institution of marriage and the family, it affirms and extends it. The editors of *The Economist* have made the same point:

> Once homosexuals can marry, will marital anarchy follow? That might be true if homosexual unions were arbitrary configurations, mere parodies of 'real' marriage. But the truth is that countless homosexual couples have shown that they are as capable of fidelity, responsibility and devotion as are heterosexual couples – and this despite having to keep their unions secret, at least until recently. Would gay marriage weaken the standard variety? There is little reason to think so. Indeed the opposite seems at least as likely; permitting gay marriage could reaffirm society's hope that people of all kinds settle down into stable unions. (6 January 1996)

It is also important to support the legal recognition of same-sex couples as a matter of social justice. As things stand, a gay couple may live together for years, but when one dies, the surviving partner may have very few rights over their home, property, or even the funeral arrangements. The experience of AIDS produced countless heartbreaking stories of gay partners, one of whom had nursed the other through sickness, being separated from one another at the deathbed and funeral by hostile parents, who in law were accorded the final right to the body of a son whom they might have rejected and ignored for years.

The ultimate importance of recognition, however, goes well beyond questions of social security or secular justice. For homosexuals there is a deeper, more inward wound to be healed, and a deeper freedom to be won, from the legacy of immemorial fear and repression. In the best sense, and at a profound level, it is a matter of gaining self-respect. Homosexuals have internalized society's rejection, and it is only society's – and even more the Church's – acceptance which can heal it. Andrew Sullivan describes the importance of establishing a recognized form of same-sex monogamy in these terms:

> It is not simply about 'taming' or 'civilizing' gay men. It is also the deepest means for the liberation of homosexuals, providing them with the only avenue for sexual and emotional development that can integrate them as equal human beings and remove from them the hideous historic option of choosing between their joy and their dignity. It is about deepening and widening and strengthening the possibility of true intimacy between two human beings. (*Love Undetectable*, p. 67)

It is, in other words, about how homosexuals can best realize their fullest humanity, their making in the image of God. The Church understands marriage as a covenant within which two people are called to find their truest selves by giving themselves away in love to one another. It is a 'mystery' or sacrament of God because it potentially reflects the mystery of self-giving love which is at the heart of the Trinity, the dynamic, creative interchange of love which binds persons in one, yet such that they become more fully themselves. At the same time, the couple are a cell in the Body of Christ, the Church, where we are all learning, often painfully and sacrificially, to live in love with each other, to understand and enter into the experience of each other, so as also to model and reflect at the level of our common life the unity-in-diversity which is the life of God. So in different ways, at different levels, both marriage and the Church are God-given training-grounds for learning Trinitarian love. Both can 'work' equally for homosexual people – if they are allowed in – because homosexual people are no less made in God's image than heterosexuals, and no less capable of loving in his image. For that reason among many others, Eugene Rogers, in a meticulous study of sexuality in relation to the Christian tradition, concludes that the explicit inclusion of homosexual couples within that Body is crucial not only to the health of homosexuals but also to the health and completeness of the Church itself.

> Gay and lesbian unions can build up the Church as well as straight marriages do, with or without children in both cases. Certainly lesbian and gay relationships can exhibit an egoism *a deux*, but they need not, any more than straight ones do. Still, marriage forms that included gay and lesbian couples would make clear that their unions, too, are from and for the larger community – indeed, if the kingdom of God is like a wedding feast, then it is thus that they too represent the Trinity. (*Sexuality and the Christian Body*, p. 273)

Formal recognition, self-acceptance, visibility, and acceptance by Church and society at large are all interdependent; each helps the others forward. But perhaps the greatest of these is visibility.

Knowing an ordinary gay couple is the best antidote to prejudice and the best way of destroying the ludicrous stereotypes and suspicions that still lurk in the mind of many. People soon come to realize the lifestyle doesn't differ much from their own. As one 'out' priest put it, 'Once it dawned on the parish that having a partner didn't mean orgies at the vicarage but having arguments about who goes to Tesco's and who walks the dog, they stopped minding. They realized we were the same as them.' Fortunately, this does seem to be the most frequent experience of clergy and others who take the risk of letting their relationships be known to those around them. It is only by helping good relationships to be seen that healing will come – for everybody.

Postscript

It would be good to end on a positive note, but that would not be true to present circumstances. While the process of recognizing and integrating homosexuals is continuing in society at large, the most visible and vocal obstacle to that process remains the Church. That is a tragedy for the Church even more than for homosexuals. The English bishops who voted for the Resolution on Human Sexuality at the Lambeth Conference, together with those in Parliament who opposed the Equalization of the Age of Consent bill and the adoption of European Human Rights legislation (largely through fear that it would give new rights to gay people), have ensured that at the start of the new millennium the Church is once again seen by gay people in this country as Enemy Number One. They have guaranteed that this particular section of the population, which needs more than most to be brought in from the margins, will be the least likely to come within its doors.

That is not new, but it had seemed that we had progressed beyond this point. Instead, Lambeth 1998 was a step backwards even from the bishops' Statement of 1991. The shock is that so many consciences were so easily suppressed, so few lessons apparently learned, so few connections drawn with the other areas, racial, social and sexual, where the Church has belatedly realized that Christ is on the side of justice. Almost as long as it has existed, the Church has been directly responsible for evils and injustices committed against homosexuals. Appalling atrocities have been perpetrated on homosexuals by the Church, or in the name of the Church, or as in Nazi Germany, with the tacit connivance of the Church. Yet there is not a glimmer of repentance; rather the opposite – an arrogant and unintelligent reaffirmation of bigotry. The much televised attempt of one bishop at the Lambeth Conference forcibly to exorcise a gay Christian leader was an iconic moment which has imprinted itself deeply in the gay psyche. It will not be quickly forgotten. Nor should the bishops imagine that the deeds of 'homophobia' can somehow be isolated from their own words and votes. They continue to supply the ideology which undergirds prejudice, and continue to bear the heaviest responsibility for it.

Questions

Introduction

1. What is your initial reaction to the words 'homo-sexual', 'lesbian', 'gay'? Before reading this booklet, where did you stand on the 'gay issue' in the Church?

2. Were you aware of the Lambeth Conference resol-ution on sexuality in 1998, or the bishops' Statement of 1991, *Issues in Human Sexuality?* Does what is said about them here surprise you?

3. Why do you think some gay people are strongly opposed to this author's view that marriage is appro-priate to gay relationships as well as to heterosexual relationships?

4. What do you think of the author's view that admit-ting gay couples into the sacrament of marriage is similar to admitting women into the sacrament of ordination?

5. Do you think that there are any gay couples in your church? Would you know? If not, why not?

6. How do you react to the author's claim that in asking to have their relationships accepted, most gay people only want what everyone else takes for granted?

Is It Scriptural?

1. What is your reaction to the story of Simon? If you had been in the vicar's place, what would you have said?

2. Do you agree with the author's claim that it is

unfair to take the Bible literally on the subject of homosexuality, but not on the subject of remarried divorcees, or the subordination of women?

3. How useful is Old Testament material which mentions homosexuality in helping us decide about it today?

4. Read Romans 1:18–end. Does the author's commentary on the passage seem fair?

5. Does it make any difference that Paul seems to think only in terms of homosexual acts committed by basically heterosexual people, and was unaware that for some people sexuality is not a matter of choice?

6. Why is it significant that Jesus and Paul do not link their call to faithfulness in marriage to practical reasons of childbearing and family stability, but to spiritual ones?

7. Do you think it is true, as the author interprets Paul and Jesus as saying, that 'sexual union always has spiritual consequences'?

8. Do you agree that a same-sex couple can 'signify the union between Christ and the Church' in the same way as a heterosexual couple? If not, what is the difference?

9. Can you conceive of a 'distinctively Christian' gay relationship? What would be distinctive about it?

Is It Moral?

1. How important is it to the moral argument that two male or two female bodies do not physically fit together?

2. The author notes a strong reaction in many people against anal intercourse in particular. Does it make any difference to the argument whether we are talking

about manual, oral or anal homosexual sex? Is it more morally acceptable if heterosexual couples also do the same things to each other?

3. Why do you think lesbianism seems to arouse less opposition in society than male gay sex?

4. What do you think of the author's comparison of the use of the body in gay sex with a handicapped person writing with his feet?

5. Do you agree that the question whether homosexuality is caused by genes or by upbringing is irrelevant to the argument about accepting gay relationships?

6. Do you agree that the fact that a gay couple cannot have children makes no difference to the argument?

7. How would you feel if your child told you he or she was gay? What would you say and do?

8. The bishops say homosexual couples can be 'a blessing to the world around them'. How?

9. Would you agree with the bishops that a homosexual relationship is necessarily less valid than a heterosexual one?

10. Do you think it is true that a man and a woman complement each other in a way that two men or two women never can?

11. This author is strongly opposed to using the term 'friendship' for a homosexual relationship, and prefers 'monogamy', 'covenant' or 'marriage'. Why?

12. How do you feel about using the words 'marriage' and 'monogamy' of a relationship between two men or two women?

13. The author is very positive and traditional in his attitude to marriage. Is he right? Or do you side with Elizabeth Stuart, believing marriage is based on

slavery, and that gay people would be better off with freer forms of relationship?

14. What do you think of the author's view that sex, gay or straight, is best kept within a faithful, lifelong relationship? Do you agree that this is a more important question than the particular question of gay relationships?

15. Do you agree with the author's view that a liberationist view of sex is 'dangerous'. Why – or why not?

Is It Achievable?

1. Are you surprised that so many homosexual relationships seem to last?

2. Do you agree that homosexual men are not inherently more promiscuous than heterosexual men? Do you agree that women (straight or lesbian) are generally less promiscuous than men?

3. How do you account for the fact that the majority of men arrested for having gay sex in public places are married?

4. This author does not discuss bisexuality. What advice would you give to a person who is equally attracted to both sexes?

5. Do you agree that promiscuous sexual activity 'tends ultimately to futility, desecration and the disintegration of the person'?

6. Are there grounds for the Church accepting lay people in a same-sex relationship, but not clergy?

7. How would you react if you discovered your vicar/priest/minister was in a gay relationship?

8. If you were a bishop or other senior Church leader, and one of your clergy told you he or she was gay, how would you react?

9. How would you feel if you were invited to a blessing service for a gay couple, or if you heard one was going to take place in your church?

10. Do you know any same-sex couples? If so, how have they influenced your view?

11. Do you think recognizing same-sex partnerships would threaten marriage and family life?

12. Do you think it is right to give same-sex couples social status and legal rights?

13. Do you agree that the Church might actually benefit from public recognition of same-sex couples?

14. How do you feel about the Church of England bishops' stand against homosexual partnerships, equalizing the age of consent, and equal employment rights?

15. Do you agree that the Church should recognize its own part in the oppression of gay people, and seek ways to redeem it?

Select Bibliography

The Gloucester Report published as *Homosexual Relationships – A Contribution to Discussion* (London, Church Information Office, 1979)

Issues in Human Sexuality: A Statement by the House of Bishops (London, Church House Publishing, 1991)

Boswell, J., *Christianity, Social Tolerance and Homosexuality* (Chicago, University of Chicago, 1980)

Bly, R., *Iron John* (London, Element, 1991)

Bradshaw, T. (ed.), *The Way Forward? Christian Voices on Homosexuality and the Church* (London, Hodder & Stoughton, 1998)

Brett, P., *Rethinking Christian Attitudes to Sex* (Colchester, University of Essex, 1991)

Cotter, J. (ed.), *Exploring Lifestyles: An Introduction to Services of Blessing for Gay Couples* (London, Gay Christian Movement, 1980)

Cotter, J., *Freedom and Framework: The Shaping of Gay Relationships* (London, Gay Christian Movement, 1978)

Countryman, L.W., *Dirt, Greed and Sex* (London, SCM, 1988)

Dominian, J., *Sexual Integrity* (London, Mowbray, 1987)

Fletcher, B., *Clergy Under Stress* (London, Mowbray, 1990)

John, J., 'Homosexuality and the Bible' in *Widening the Horizons* (London, Christian Action, 1990)

Kelly, K.T., *New Directions in Sexual Ethics* (London, Geoffrey Chapman, 1998)

McNeill, J., *The Church and the Homosexual* (New York, Next Year, 1985)

Moore, G., *The Body in Context: Sex and Catholicism* (London, SCM, 1992)

Nelson, J., *The Intimate Connection: Male Sexuality, Masculine Spirituality* (London, SPCK, 1992)

Rogers, E.F., *Sexuality and the Christian Body* (Oxford, Blackwell, 1999)

Sanderson, T., *Making Gay Relationships Work* (London, Other Way, 1990)

Stuart, E., *Daring to Speak Love's Name* (London, Hamish Hamilton, 1992)

Just Good Friends (London, Mowbray, 1995)

Sullivan, A., *Virtually Normal* (London, Picador, 1995)

Same-sex Marriage: Pro and Con. A Reader (New York, Random House, 1997)

Love Undetectable (London, Chatto & Windus, 1998)

Tessina, T., *Gay Relationships* (Los Angeles, Tarcher, 1989)

Thatcher, A., *Liberating Sex*: A Christian Sexual Theology (London, SPCK, 1993)

Thévenot, X., *Homosexualités Masculines et Morale Chrétienne* (Paris, Cerf, 1985)

Vasey, M., *Evangelical Christians and Gay Rights* (Nottingham, Grove Books, 1991)

Strangers and Friends: A New Exploration of Homosexuality and the Bible (London, Hodder & Stoughton, 1995)

Wenham, G., 'Homosexuality in the Bible' in T. Higton (ed.), *Sexuality and the Church* (Action for Biblical Witness to Our Nation) (Eastbourne, Kingsway, 1987)

Williams, H., *Poverty, Chastity and Obedience* (London, Mitchell Beazley, 1975)